For Janet –

An amazing person

who is —

Fully Human

With love

by
Samuel P. Magill

June 2013

Manufactured in the United States of America

Design: PIXELS

Library of Congress Catalog Card Number: 2006902015

Intenational Standard Book Number: 0-9779270-0-8

Cover Art: Solstice Day Mimes, Seattle, WA, Photograph by Samuel P. Magill
Photography by Samuel P. Magill, except where noted.

The poem Earth Homework was previously published in Developing A Public Faith,
2003 Richard R. Osmer and Friedrich L. Schweitzer, eds. Chalice Press, St. Louis,
Missouri. Copyright retained by author.

Contents

To friends everywhere
through whom I have learned
what it means to be human.

Acknowledgements...

The fact that you are holding this small volume of poems is a miracle of relationships. The book exists only because some very special friends called it forth from my reluctance and denial of being a poet. Mary, my friend and wife of 31 years, lead the effort by calling first on one, then on more and more people, whom she knew I trusted, to corral my resistance and she deserves the biggest thanks. David Robinson, Megan Schopf, Terri Anderson and Rick Stone came to my house to encourage me. They are four muses in human form who helped me understand that their love has room for all of my gifts and curses. In the process, Megan created a visual image of her experience of me in the pastel drawing called "The Man With the Flowing Heart" that hangs on my office wall. Whenever I find myself in doubt, I turn to the powerful images in her drawing and draw much strength.

The next circle of friends met at Claude's house on the shore of beautiful Lake Tahoe in January, 2004. There, Megan, David, Patty Thibault, Diane Bush and Laura Abernathy extracted a promise from me to collect my poems into one place just to see how many there were. Diane Branson created "fire talks" in which she regularly held my feet to the fire, melting yet another bit of resistance. Kathleen Stinnett received an early complete collection and read a few poems at a time so she could savor them and even now a year later continues to take them in from time to time. Her saying some of the lines brought smiles and tears was the best sort of encouragement. Good people of the Hudson Institute in Santa Barbara, both leadership team and participants, said the poems mattered to them—even folks who said they didn't read poetry. Equally important, Larry Parks Daloz was the first to read one of the poems, "Earth Homework," in a public setting and Sharon Daloz Parks included it first in an article and then a book. Sharon also led me to Ann Medlock who introduced me to Susan Reed who took the raw material and made it look like a book. David Robinson helped select photos from my own collection and offered an artist's eye to the whole effort. David is also responsible for several poems by sending early morning emails in which he told me the universe expected a poem that day.

There are others: The people who were polite enough to listen, David Whyte who unknowingly set much in motion through his work with Boeing Executives and his book, *The Heart Aroused*. Elizabeth Cohen who so gently called for me to let my heart show. David Sluyter and Mickey Olivanti of the Fetzer Institute who provided the means and occasions for me to meet most of these wonderful people. Diane Goldin continues to call me to ask how long the world has to wait for this collection – I've got to get her off my back so she can move on to other worldly challenges. Diane Connelly whose constant calling is for us to embrace life exactly as it is. Mary Shehane may possibly have saved my life by listening and by taking my lamentations more seriously than I did and Gina Rembeisa, who helped me say 'yes' not just to life in general, but specifically my own. And there are more of you, unnamed.

Why *Fully Human*? Part of my resistance to collecting and publishing these words is that they are self revealing. One early reader, Max, said he felt he was reading my private journal. You are right, Max. Each poem reflects my interaction or perception of a moment in time. Some are deeply personal, looking inside my own being. Some of those expose considerable depression, anxiety or longing. Some reveal my love of my family, my delights and struggles in being a father. Some reflect my desire to be of use and my half-deaf listening to God.

Now I am convinced that our primary task is to become fully human. We need not look very far away, but somehow, as Irish writer—poet John O'Donohue has suggested we make the short physiological trip to our hearts very arduous indeed. All of our strivings—our American addiction to advancement and "moving up a level"—are disguised efforts to be accepted as we are—just as we are.

The key moment in which I turned toward gathering these poems came one morning at that meeting at Lake Tahoe. Through some means, we had all gathered at dawn and as I looked at my still sleepy friends and myself in our pajamas and bed-head hair, I found my favorite lines in all these poems:

> First waking in rumpled hair,
> Having not put on my beauty masks
> Or prepared myself for public viewing,
> Will I allow myself to be called,
> Beloved?

If we can say yes to that query, I say we have reached a milestone in becoming fully human.

Similarly, in a moment of doubt about my value as a person, husband, father, friend, worker, I said to God as I fell asleep that He should take my life and give it to someone who would cherish it and do with it what He intended. In the days that followed, I found Him saying that, indeed, He had given my life to the person He trusted most. What could be better confirmation of my place among humanity?

So, now, I offer you these poems knowing some are better than others and hoping that even one line will somehow open a door for you to embrace your own humanness.

Belize. Christmas 2005

Human Beings

In 2004, I had the great joy of volunteering to support the Council for a Parliament of the World's Religions in Kenya and Spain. My role, along with immensely talented colleagues from around the world, was to facilitate conversations about the plight of refugees. The objective of the dialog was to initiate "simple and profound" acts in the participants' own communities. It was truly a global event and I received far more than I gave. The first three poems emerged from that experience. The remainders reflect thoughts about being human and being human in relationship with God.

The Parliament meetings

What more can be said?
We met and talked with people
from around the world.
We met and used too many words
to say all that needed to be said.

We from the west and north.
have our strategies and methods
but in the end what matters
Is the look in each other's eyes,
the question asked at the right
time because we have listened
or because we took the time to breathe.

They were our teachers.
We, the students, were the ones
who received so much
by being in their presence.

I ask if I did my best.
and there is only "no"
because it was not I who did
anything but the one
who sent me
and I ache knowing
there is nothing to do
except open my heart.

I receive blessings
from people more wise,
more present
more fully engaged each day
in their own faiths
and they astound me.

Now I know and fear
what faith can do and
what it demands.
Those who are making a difference
are the ones whose lives are
wrapped in love of which
they never speak
who may never be noticed
or paid a dime.

Unimaginable possessions

We have touched people
from around the entire world
and been touched by their eyes,
their hands, their hearts.
Mine breaks again and again
knowing how small I am
and how much time I seem to spend
on my own survival instead
of reaching out to them regardless
of what I have,
knowing I have far more possessions
than they can even dream of
much less desire.

And I feel tainted by my own possessions
even as I seek ways to maintain them.
Afraid, in fact, that I am not as strong as the
young refugee from Columbia,
the doctor fleeing from Cuba,
the monks forbidden from going home,
the Kenyan uncle whose sister
is dying with AIDS while he
stays home to care for her children,
the devoted Nigerian working
day and night to help his neighbors
simply live, and the sisters from across
the Middle Eastern wall who each feared
in the night they might be killed by the other
until they recognized their own fear
in the other's eyes and fell into each others' arms.

The Sihks who served 30,000 meals only
because they love each stranger at their door
and if there were not enough strangers they
went looking for us and fed us
at whatever hour we appeared
asking us only to wash our hands
and cover our heads in that most
holy of holy places where food is served.

And in the end all I can say, like Jesus
to the rich young man—
"Sell every thing and give it to the poor"
who already have possessions I
cannot imagine.

Institutions of Faith

All over the world governments are fighting,
justifying their wars,
their business,
their self-defense
and they have been doing so
for a thousand years—
more even than that.

All over the world people are hungry
people are homeless
people thirst for more than water
and that also.

All over the world religious institutions
study their scripture for guidance
hoping to find some way through
the dark time of human experience
hoping for some kind of divine revelation
and their disciples defend the text
with their lives, forgetting
what the saints were seeking
at the beginning.

Meanwhile,
all over the world there are people
in twos and threes who have gone to
the depths of their faiths
seeking only to know how to live,
how to love,

and, if they are lucky,
how to organize their lives for
some purpose beyond themselves,
knowing that each breath they
breathe is the same breath sought
by countless others in far off places
they will never see.
And, yet, they know the sound of each
one's heart beat because it is their own.

All over the world,
people in twos and threes
are drawing what they can from
their wells of living water
handing out cups to slake
each other's thirst.
They do not wait for governments
or institutional seers to find the way.
They already know because they
have listened to the sound of childrens'
hunger and looked into the eyes
of kind strangers.

They know they have no time to
loose and the task is more
than they can possibly do.
But they do not stop except
to gather their breath again
and call each other to silence,
to silence, and prayer and service.

In the end, no government will
withstand the steady growing
call to wholeness of all humanity.
Each person of the same value
and merit.
Each person loved by and loving
those who walk the human road beside them.

Institutions of Faith. Parliament of the World's Religions. Montserat, Spain. July 2004.

Strange Creatures |

We are strange creatures, we humans;
by nature seeking newness, conquest, treasure.
We have explored all corners of the earth,
discovered strange and wonderful beings
who share this place in the universe.
We have followed the longest river
and sailed the largest ocean—
even hurtled across space to distant moons.
Our ships have visited mars and the sun
and our telescopes extend our view
toward the cosmic edge.

Yet we are not satisfied.
We search beyond what we know,
discomforted by what we do not,
as if some ancient beast still roamed
in wilderness before us,
threatening our village, our loved ones
our knowledge and security.

Will we ever rest, we humans?

Long ago we were told and told again
the kingdom of our longing
was at hand, with no need to voyage
beyond our reach.

We doubt it still and this is our diversion—
to think that what we seek is
over there
under there
out there,

while answers wait untapped inside
the very place we already inhabit,
waiting for us to recognize our homes
where nothing is missing,
where what we know or have been told
is just enough to live—
and truly living is our hearts' real desire.

Strange Creatures II

Our goal, our mission, if we chose
is not some far off place,
some continent or star,
but close at hand—
just over there next to us.
If only we would turn our heads toward
our hearts and see each other
already where we long to be,
the kingdom of our heart's desire
waiting here and now.

Here and now in a child's eyes
in a friend
in a stranger
in our partner long ignored
whose eyes we lost in our desire
to explore beyond our knowing,
to fill ourselves with stimulus
to remind us that we live.

What proof do we need
that we are loved just as we are
and perfectly formed in this moment
full and living,
a territory and a miracle no farther off
than now?

We humans are a strange creation
we have capacities to learn,
to question, and to seek
but are we made to call enough enough?

Leaving Mumbai

Hungry mama.
Hungry baby.
Where will you sleep tonight, beggar mother?
Where will your baby rest its tiny head?
Will there be warmth?
Is there love in your house?

You walk among
    cars,
        mopeds,
            buses,
                bicycles,
                    elephants.
Is this your garden, your park?

Dear India do you see?
You turn your face
while she taps my window
with enough English words
to crush my heart
(How desperately we need strangers in our
lives to see what we no longer notice).
You, kind hostess, turn your face
and go back to your guarded home,
while I fly home—safe, warm, loved.

Who are you India?
You serve me by asking me
to hold all the opposites of life
and still say welcome.
Who's to say there is pain?
Who's to say life is hard?
I no longer know what hard is.
I see you in a tattered shack – the local
barber shop where old men
laugh drinking chai.

Children laugh,
lovers secretly love,
local culture decries sensuality,
and AIDS is spreading,
and the government is corrupt
and the courts are cleaning it up
again.

There's more going on than
meets the stranger's eye,
and life beats and moves
relentlessly.

The voice of God

We have no need to fear
all the voices of humanity.
In combination the melodies and
cadences blend, rising and
falling deep and light blending
I am sure into something like
the song of angels.

There is one song with different voices,
each one a note:
"A" is rich only in its difference
from other notes
and only together are they music.

We are so richly blessed by and for each other.
Light cannot know light without the dark
as a forest of oak would need no name to call itself.
No two people are perfectly alike—
our differences make us what we are—
each fitting into the puzzle called humanity.

The moment full contact with others comes,
we can never go back to being separate.
When the many become one song,
we are touched by our one human heart and
there is no recovery.

Listen to the song
perhaps together we are the voice of God!

Folk Life Festival. Seattle, Washington. May 2005.

New Orleans Airport, 2003
– sitting with God

I don't know why they come any more –
the workers lost in daily sameness,
such sadness, division, desperation—
no meaning except the somewhat,
sometimes adequate pay.

Meanwhile, those of us who've met
our basic needs talk of calling,
and working toward our highest purpose.
yet we, too, long for more.

What we really want
is to touch the unseeable something
that we can never fulfill, or own, or be,
to transcend ourselves, to be
in the presence of something unknowable:
fierce, burning, reassuring in its very
strangeness and uncontrollable wild mystery.

Times gone by we lived and found our purpose
on the border of the place beyond the veil.
That was before science, before technology,
before knowing so much that wild
yearning was removed.
We thought we would find God
or at least tame creation
(out of longing to have no fear).

But seeing our thirst to grasp full knowledge,
God moved a little farther away,
making existence that much larger—
this shy creator still not wanting
fully to be known.

If everything is known, there is no quest,
no need for art, for poetry,
for unspeakable love and
when all is within our grasp,
we get bored, indulging all our appetites
yet never being filled or nourished.

So, loving God moves out a bit,
knowing that our longing keeps us living.
Each apple of knowledge
we pluck from the tree makes us bigger
but brings us no closer to real creation.

Perhaps if we rested from time to time
God too could rest,
as shepherds do when the flock is home.
Then, sitting once again down in the garden,
we would see God just beyond the trees.
We both would nod and smile,
feasting on the riches of the day
(having both won our game of hide and seek)
Tomorrow we would play again,
until our mother-father calls us home
to rest one final time, forever.

So long as we shall seek
and hearts shall grow
so long lives God
beyond all that we know.

Beloved

First waking in rumpled hair
having not adorned myself
for public viewing
or put on my beauty masks –
will I allow myself to be
called Beloved?

Dark Journey

In 1996, I was in a great and cranky state, so much so that I told my self I was not sure I should go on living. Diane Connelly, who taught me to bow to life, acknowledging it exactly as it is, suggested I follow the traditions of some cultures that, when facing death, the person writes his or her death song. When I returned from a meeting in Scottsdale, where I wrote such a poem, Diane invited me to read it to a group. What astounded me was that the words touched a good many people who in one way or another had talked with death. We were far less alone in these conversations than one would think and, having shared the dark words, we then talked about life with great appreciation.

I offer the following poems to all who have taken a dark journey or suffered, like Saint John of the Cross, a very dark night of the soul. That voyage is part of the human experience and only its denial or its unguided experience are damaging.

Roosting tree at sunrise. Marasimba Lodge. Masai Mara, Kenya. March 2004.

Cold night in Scottsdale

You came to me again.
That cold January night,
your now familiar door
opened, beckoning,
promising an end to agony,
to wishing life were different than it is
…..so easy to step through,
my place already set, waiting.
The dance would end –
stillness, quiet, no more relating.
Just one step to end it all.

Must you linger so close?
Your cold breath
always on one cheek?
My bones and flesh are
drawn to the four directions,
the four sacred mountains so
thunderously silent, so
searingly cold even
the cloudless sky at noon
cannot warm me.

Will there come a day when I say welcome
and fall into you with one last aahhhh
releasing all, returning to the infinite
where no two exist?
No like-dislike.

No right-wrong.
No good-bad.
No love-hate.
No dark-light.
No day-night.
No sleep-awake.
Pure is, pure now, pure forever.

Will I fall in like a worker coming home
from a long day's labor,
or will you arrive unspoken
and snatch away the chance
to say YES to life once more?
Are you friend or foe?
Can I know before I choose
to take that last, tempting step?

In praise of poets

I thank you poets for warmth of heart,
for courage in the dark,
for speaking what cannot be said.
Homer, Virgil, Robert, David,
Emily, Marge, May,
Rumi, Hafiz, John, Pablo,
Antonio, Reiner,…
You light my path and warm my soul.
You guide me in the dark
and reach inside my heart
when no one else can.
You who have traveled
the depth of human existence—
perhaps of all existence—
and come back to tell the story.

Mid winter

It truly is mid winter now.
Darkness is pervasive and
and bare limbs sway silently
in a motionless cold breeze.
One solitary bird takes flight
as I step into the garden.
Red twigs stand starkly
against the deep green cedar.
The great empress tree
lifts her branches imploring heaven for sun.

But in the midst of this semi-permanent gloom,
there stands the winter witch hazel,
refusing not to bloom.
In defiance of the dark
she shares her yellow bits
of light and sweet, sweet smell.
This also is our task:
to stand with grace and loving light
as antidote to all that darkens life.

Winter Witch-hazel. Magill backyard. January 2006.

I once believed

I once believed in God
Who created heaven and earth
And held each of us in His hand.
I still do sort of believe
In the one who sets
The stars and each of us in motion,
In the one who gives us comfort
When the times of pain arrive,
Or when the magnificent sunset speaks
Of life eternal.

But the respondent God
Who listens to us and acts
At our behest
Now leaves me cold.
I do not pray for special grace
For brother, sister, child, spouse
Or healing when I know
We all must die.

Still, dear God, please use me well
And tell me how and whom to serve,
So when I breathe my last
I rest in peace.

Post Modern Blues

Which one of us will never die?
Which one of us knows the truth?

In our times we're told
There's none of the assurances of old
When truth was cut
From just one mould.
Now, each thought is ours,
The fabric of our own creation.

We have perfected science
Yet we are more and more afraid.

Are we not made of earth,
As God made Adam from a bit of mud?
Of mud and water, air and fire.
In all our modern surety
We still are subject to eternity.

Old brown rivers carry mud from mountains,
Granite cliffs are cut by ice,
Pacific islands grow with fire,
Southwest rocks are formed by wind.

Who among us is separate from that truth?

The Sweat Lodge

Black, hot silent womb
alone, melting, dripping, dark.
Black, hot steaming womb,
drumming heart beat songs.
Black, hot, sweating womb.
Prayers of healing
Prayers of service.
Black, hot sacred womb
Birthing love and life.

The sound of my own silence

I listen for the sound of my own silence
and cannot find it.
Clanging thoughts and images shroud
every crevice of my heart.
My mind is full of distractions:
the voices in the hall,
the pretty feet of the woman next to me,
a distant bird, a plane, the tea kettle,
the sound of pens and paper stirring,
a bell some where else
calling someone else
to their work.

I listen to the sound of others' breathing.
(Near me there is a doctor
who knows the sound of her patients'
more than the sound of her own heart.)
but here is also my own silence.

Just now there was a moment
of peace between two thoughts—
a second or two when
I connected without thought
with the food
left on the table
the fragrance of a flower
and scent of some soft perfume.
My own silence
From which my senses
Touch the world.

The play at Rendezvous hut

Je suis content.
The gas lantern hushes,
shhhhh, like an usher
waiting for the play to begin.
The stage is set with candle glow,
warm food settling in
now that we have eaten.

Outside
the dark cold world rests,
comforted in its snowy down.
Peace and quiet surround the hut as
all of nature waits for life to stir.

It is much more quiet out than in
where my chattery mind
keeps interrupting both the player
and those who witness
Winter's quiet silent drama.

The usher keeps at me,
until, thought by city thought
I let the world slip away
content to be on this stage
where only the silence
speaks its lines.

Salmon Carcass

Remember all the horror stories
about how goodness is so often
carried off by ghouls?
Evil cannot hide. Listen:

You know the eagle that took
the salmon carcass?
It was beautiful.....
head, guts and bones—death
carried off on wings.

Lost Soul – Breitenbush

Last Winter,
I went far a field to find my soul.
It was lost among still waters of the forest.
They were deep and silent
in the snow frosted morning
but warmed by earth's fire
far below the seasons.

I remember traveling long ago
searching for God knows what.
This longing is not new.

But this year I stayed home
and found my soul
where it had always been.
Here, now, I am home
and am found.

Incarcerated in work

Cage doors slam shut
and I cry freedom!
Tastes of wild weekend paths
remain looming up like giant trees
blowing in the wind.
Clothing smells of fire.
Sweet sore muscles remember
freedom.

Now smoke—a different sort—
clouds the office corridor
and bad coffee spills
from modern convenience gadgets;
wherr of fans create
the only trace of wind.
Prison.

Emigrant Gap – 10,000 Feet

Just after noon we entered heaven—
each small stone
each tiny leaf and flower
spoke perfection in the mid-day sun.

By one we had entered hell.
The perfection went on and on.
We marched for hours
and nothing changed.
Pure torture!

Nothing

We all get to this point
when we long to write
or speak, or paint,
or dance and
there is nothing.

Pens poised leave no mark,
mouths open with no sound,
brushes rest in the tray,
feet stick where they are.

The universe called me
for a poem today,
disturbed by all this quiet—
it's own muse sleeping
through these dark days.
No word, image, movement
to express this absence
of everything
but silence.

Alone without Virgil

Last night I dreamed I woke
in Dante's darkened woods
without good Virgil's hand
to take me where I could not go
alone.

Then I heard voices near and far
saying we will go with you.
and I asked who they were.

Friends, just friends, who before
and after you will travel the same road,
there's only one after all.

These strange friends who would
spend a part of their lives on my behalf,
I asked them why.
They said because we love you.

Dangerously boxed

Sitting in my study, angry
I think about trashing the images around me
all constructed to look good.
Instead, I lock the living part of me away.

In my mind I run
springing across meadows
falling down in tall grass and
making love with the wild woman
living unrestrained,
my powerful mind and will at work
not fearing what might happen,
boldly leading simply to lead
to feel the power of followers,
saying at last, I am.

Fearing my sense of power as sinful,
fearing my mind and lust for life
I lock the exciting part of me
dangerously in a box,
slide it underground,
under earth,
out of site—
not out of mind.

Lioness. Masai Mara. Kenya. March 2004.

Death you are too easy

Death, you are too easy, too clear.
This body will end.
Period.

It's not death that's hard but life where
living calls to us,
demanding we show up
today and again
in all the tomorrows
until the end.

Family and Friends

Can we possibly over state the importance of family and friends? Greeting cards are inclined toward either syrupy sentiment or silly sayings, but relationships of all sorts are so much more than that. Nothing, absolutely nothing, is ever done completely on our own. The rugged American individualist, the John Wayne corporate CEO, rides on the shoulders of people he never even sees. We must begin to understand that at the end of our lives, the very best stories are about the people we have loved and who have loved us. In much of modern life, love is trivialized – even described as "touchy-feely" in some "tough minded" organizations. When I worked at Boeing, I learned through the communication grapevine, that one manager referred to the leadership team meetings I helped convene as "Sam's love-ins." I was greatly wounded. Now I know he was right. And so was I.

At Claude's House

May all who dwell in this house
be blessed by the loving hands that created it.
May they be blessed by the earth that offered
itself in wood and stone and fiber.
May they be blessed by the sun that rises and
sets above it.
May they be blessed by the art created in it
and the birds keeping watch by day and night;
by black bear visiting in the dark.
May all who share this space be well tended
by the spirit who dwells here every day
and by us souls who visit from time to time.
May hearts be warmed by love expressed
here over and over again.
May they be enriched by the offering of him
who called this place into being.
Finally, may these visitors
each further enrich this house by their love
and at their parting, may they give thanks
for all they have received.
May this house endure long into time.

A lonely loving dream

Last night I had a dream.
Like many, it was mixed
loneliness and love together
leading one first, then the other.
Losing you in crowds
loving you at the station
losing you in madness
loving you and saying I do
again and again and again.

Knowing my own shape

How gladly I accept your partnership
in this good work and breathe in fully
the air and water to fill my own shape,
My own shape that I was in all along
and did not know.

Like the far out sea that does not know
its own vast form, it has no sight of the land
from which it gains its shape.

By our meeting and our differences
my own shape grew clear.

Soul friend

This friendship of the soul
fills my heart with light
and leads my scattered mind
to depth and stillness
I have seldom known.

Your eyes shine through me
knowing what even I
have not seen in myself—
a perfect knowing held
with grace that amazes me
in every fresh moment.

I delight in your smile
with a sweet joy
that needs no explanation.
and yet, I am also greedy—
wanting to clutch, to possess
as Tolkien's Gollum jealously
sought the ring of power.
Mine, only mine.

Still,
if I put on that ring of power
both of us would disappear;
and so I ease myself
into the sweetness of
the untouched space
between and guard it
with my heart.

Beowulf's Sword

The old stories guild our history
with gold and armor
and tales of great deeds,
of skill and power,
of swords' authority gained
through a lineage of hands held by
heroes and their steeds.

Underneath the valor,
love of others won the day—
Beowulf himself did not
Succeed by broad sword's steel alone
but by his brave heart's love
against the hate and malice
of his world.

So now, do we unsheathe
our swords whose high tech
lineage to assembly lines
offers no kinsman's confidence,
no history of love
offering life's best?

Can our own foes be fought with such steel?
Is it blood and sinew, bone and flesh
opposing us in battle?
The real wars now are fought by relentless
loving and loving until there is no more hate.
This sword's lineage belongs to all of us,
forged in the fires that make all humans kin.

Before it's too late

Hurry, before it is too late,
say, "I love you",
say, "You are my friend."

Before the day is past,
let it be known that we were here,
together.
We shared this moment in time.
No one else ever in all creation
will share what we have shared.
No one else in all creation
will see what we have seen.

How sweet, how sad that time is ruthless,
that we shall not pass this way again.
We would be cheapened
if there were reruns,
if we mirrored someone who
had done all this before.

Let us rejoice that we have known
and been known,
a knowing that will never die,
will never say,
"I wonder who you were."
We have been here together
in the creation of time.
We are friends,
Now and ever.

Dialog with my paralytic self

What is the paralytic part?
  My heart.
What is up with my heart?
  It is in a cage.
What purpose does the cage offer?
  Safety.
From what?
  Embarrassment, disappointment, failure,
  commitment.
Have you ever released it before?
  When I chose a path of peace, followed
  what God asked of me.
What happened?
  I felt I lost everything, had to hide.
From what?
  The power people.
That was then, this is now.
  I know, but I am afraid.
Of what?
  Of leaping and falling.
Perhaps you can fly!
  I'm paralyzed.
How's your faith?
  My friends have great confidence and
  would do anything to see my heart soar.
So what's stopping you?
  Perhaps they are wrong.
So many? God doesn't fake love.
  I love them so much their faith heals me.
  They are God's face.
  I will leap.

The call I most fear

So near to losing you.
I still can't get my mind around
the sound of breaks
a gasp knowing this is it.
unbelievable impact
glass breaking
spinning
stopping.

Swaying upside down
the roof now on the ground
alive
out
safe.

Hitch hiker in Navajo Nation

I know this place.
These are not just rocks.
They tell the story
of my people
who have lived here
from beyond time.

> Why would these crazy people live
> out here in this heat?
> How could anybody want to be here?
> Hot, geez the bugs are bad.
> Nothing to eat.
> No water.

I pick the willow berries for breakfast,
squeezing out the tiny seeds
until I have enough
to make my coffee.

> Why not gather and sell them?

Sell them?
They were planted here for us.
We did not grow them.

> Might you leave?

I know the rocks, each one.
If I leave I will
not know the place.

Rocks breathe so slowly
we must listen for an eternity
to know what they know,
see what they see.
Their eyes are older than the hills.
They were born long
before earth's thrusting up
bore this land above the sea.

They were here long enough
for all this sand to be ground
one unbelievably small grain
at a time.

Leave?
Where could I find
that kind of patient home?

Endless Fire

Tom laid his hand on my shoulder, smiled.
"You look so camp hardened,
so, I don't know, at ease
like you've been here before."

Indeed this fire,
this air tinged with wood smoke,
the dying sun on high snow fields'
craggy rocks.
This soft new moss underfoot –
sleep's perfect mattress.

This is early summer's friendship
this eternal camp.
The same sounds I heard
with my father long ago.
Same water, same sun, same rocks
Same forest floor, same bugs.

Einstein told us time is curved.
I say it isn't there at all.

A Father's letting go

I let go of you a little bit today
and saw you less through my eyes,
perhaps a bit through yours.

In the core of your being
I trust you completely,
not as I would have you be,
but as God made you.
You beyond your body,
you beyond everything
I see and know.

Today, I bow to you deeply,
to you as you truly are,
and in bowing
renew my promise
to be Here,
to be with you
to let you be
no matter what.

Grave news

Surges of sadness course
through my body,
down the passages of grief
carved by other grave news.

There has been much death in my house,
so I am ever vigilant for her voice
and not much surprised when she comes,
but I do not relish her call and
am no less sad when she arrives
for the friend of a friend.

Still, there is some goodness
in this grave dance
ending in our essence.

You, love, are what is left
when all else slips away.
You, the great promise
and the good news.

Où Sont Mes Parents ?

Où est mon père qui aimait les montagnes?
Où est ma mère qui aimait la mer?
Toutes les eaux du monde coulent—
Des grandes océans,
Des lacs de montagne,
Des petites rivières,
Des goûttes de pluie.
Où sont mes parents?
Ils sont toujours en train
De retourner a la source
Comme toutes les sources de vie.

Touching

Touch me
That I might know
My body still exists,
That I have not made it up today.

Touch me
So I know our love
Is more than thought.

Touch me
To remind me
Even when leaves fall,
Even when snow flies,
We are still together.

I long so to be re-membered
To know that I am known,
To know life still exits
And moves beyond my loneliness.

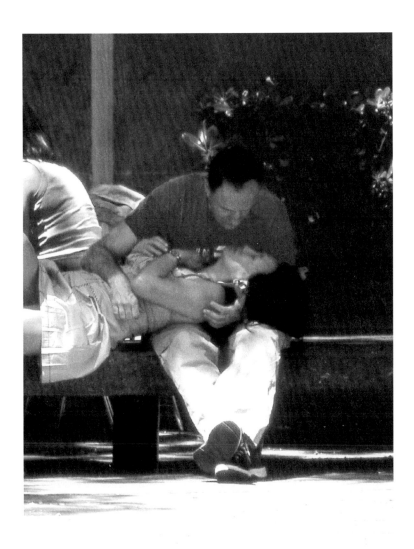

Plaza of Barcelona Cathedral. Barcelona, Spain. July 2004.

Eileen at 7

You turned seven just the other day
and got lots of pretty things—
earrings, watch, necklace—
all the stuff that makes your friends take note.

There's much, much more to life.
As years arrive, my friend,
remember that the outside
Is a package.
And the glitter of the wrapping?
Remember what happens on
Christmas Day with all the torn up paper?
The next day all that's left of glitter
is the goodness of the gift it used to hide.

I love you for whom you are inside—
a beauty which no jewel can hide,
nor nasty, jealous friends deride.

While I'm away

Look at the moon each night
And we shall be seeing the same moon.
Look at the sun
And we shall be seeing the same sun.
Pray and listen and we will
Be at one with the same God.
Breathe and we will inspire the same spirit.
For if we are in one creation
We are never apart.

Unfrozen

I listen to the parts of me
Reaching out of their souls
Each one touching the unseen
Unknown, unspoken unity among us.
I am the fish leaping from the sea.
I am the reptile self protecting.
I am the woman dousing gas
And lighting a match to take herself away.
I shoot in angry self defense and
Lose myself in the bloody snow—
Cold and starkly beautiful.
And I am the tree crashing
Next door in the woods.

The world in me and out there
Is unfrozen now, known forms
Dissolving from their comfortable shapes.

I miss the simplicity of small town
White America where I grew up,
though I knew at the time it was cruel.

So I'm planning to escape
To what?
Under my pale, oatmeal
Seattle-summer-less skin
I am many people.
I don't know them well.
Do they know me?
Do they know something about me
I may not want to hear?

Waiting room

Sitting in the waiting room,
John, a volunteer, greets the old
Gray haired lady who guards
This anxious place with love.

People pass   ,
Concerned faces glance away,
And new comer volunteers ask
For tours to learn their trade.
What ministry of love!

Puzzles set out partly built
Inviting friends whose friends' bodies
Are being reassembled or repaired
Just down the hall.

Would you like some coffee, tea or peace?
What's your name so I can find
You when there's news in
This not so anxious place?
What ministry of love!

Water, Some Distinctions

I came by the warm pools today
Down by the winter river.
Slowly undressed, climbed in.
I saw the trees, heard sounds,
Felt without touching another soul's
Gentle movements in the other pool,
My own tub's bubbles, bottom—usual stuff.
Then I leaned forward, nose to water.
As if for the first time, I saw the surface
 – the pool looked back at me.

It too was alive, with it's own form, its own soul.
This warming bath, quiet reflection of my world,
Showing me my own form, darkly shadowed in
its looking glass.

We were very very still,
As two lovers first time lock their gaze.

I've heard it said you put your hand in water,
Pull it out, the water doesn't care,
Goes back the way it was.
Not so this deep pool.
Having touched each other—
The images held below and above—
We both changed,
One languishing in the depths
One living in the outer world
Finally, reunited twins.

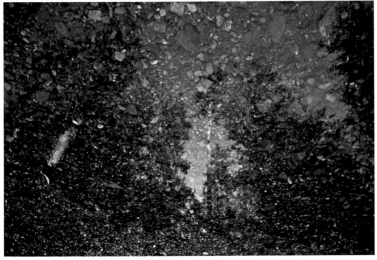

Reflective Pool. Vancouver Island, British Columbia, Canada. August 2004.

Cassal Hut

This is also enough,
This being with friends
Whose hearts are open,
Whose eyes glisten
As they tell their stories.

This food is enough
Because it is made of love.

This wood fire warms
Like no other – built
And kindled only
Because we are here.

If we had not loved
Each other enough
To arrive, the fire would
Never have been built.

Leaving

There is so much I want to say
About being here in this life
That lasted a few days or forever—
I don't remember how long
We have been here.
It doesn't matter.

Words do not suffice.
Saying "Mountain" pales by comparison
To the crystals and rocks
And lights and ice
And trees and water
That make it up.
Saying "Water" fails to describe
The sea and its depth
And breadth and waves
And currents and surface
And bottom.
Saying "friend" is too small a word
To reflect our bonds
And circle of hands.

Even saying "Love" cannot hold all
That is in my heart and yours,
In our eyes and smiles
Our warmth and truth.

With no words
I bow in silence to say
All that could be said.

Healing with time

I see my life in deepening clarity,
Each circle lowering into
The joy of knowing and each circle
Raising new questions.

Now we are 50 or 60 or more.
Old grievances drop away where once they
Were mountains and fierce storms.
Friends track down old connections
To seek and offer forgiveness
And we walk free, cleansed
Adolescent wounds healing at last.

Emergence

"Like spring's demand of blossoms", sooner or later we emerge into the world. In the Inferno, Dante Alighieri tells us that the way through the very pit of hell is to dive even deeper in faith; at that moment we emerge into light. If we have done well in the dark times, we arise like the very resurrection itself. On the other hand, if we have never experienced the dark, or "death's other self" as Shakespeare described the descent into autumn and winter, we can hardly appreciate the dawn. These poems attempt to reflect that relentless and welcome renewal, that moment when we say "YES" to life again.

View from 30,000 Feet

The old river bends its way
Across the landscape, curving
More and more until the bends
Come full circle back to themselves.
Old curves and deviations slowly fill
And dry while the main flow
Moves on down the river to
Its destination.

So are we shaped by deviations
From our main calling
The moment we move aside
In the tempting side channels
Of our lives.

Yet always, always,
We have the chance to come round
To our true selves,
Turning toward home
Again and again.

No time to be a hare

Snakes have it easy
and snow hares
and chameleons—
seasons change,
they shed their skin and coats,
grow new ones fitting the occasion.

Ah poor us.
What you see is what you get.
Unless…
unless we stop and peel ourselves back,
refitting to our change-ed world.

But that takes time and I'm in a hurry.

Upstart spring

How quickly spring consumes
The peace of winter,
Though we had prayed it would arrive soon.

Letters unsent, poems half
Written in the slow time
Now lie scattered on my desk, vague
Memories of grand intentions
When time stood still on soft or
Frosty winter mornings
And the cold nights bundled us to the fire.

Upstart spring shows
No tolerance for reflection;
Everything is in ascending motion
And if I stop to write that letter
Or pen a few more lines,
Then the weeds and grass and
Work crying to be done
Creep under the door,
Grab hold of my thoughtful moment
And drag it relentlessly to the light.

We had wanted springs' blossoms—
Their delicate scents and bright colors
A longed for departure from winter's gloom—
But just now I felt myself longing in turn
For that other time.

Bud Leaves

Finally, the buds in the apple trees
Have cracked open
Beginning their journey toward ripe fruit
In blasts of pink and white.
As days and weeks go by bees,
With luck, will do their business
And small but unambiguous apples will appear.

But before we drive ahead to harvest
Shall we not stop to notice, at least,
Or profoundly thank the case of hard
Bud leaves that protected
Our blossoms from ice, wind and mold
Through the long silent winter?

That case, perfectly designed for its task,
Held both the reality of harsh days and
Vision of sweet fruit.
It did not shrink from its task
And when it was done,
Fell silently to the ground,
Only to be consumed by the very nature
It cultivated and opposed.

Light enough

The world feels dark to me today
And yesterday was without light.

Just the other day I was in light
In mountains that serve no purpose
Other than to reflect that light
And the sound of wind and water;
Mountains that can be walked upon
With the dry crunch of andicite;
Wind that can be felt softly
In the morning breeze.

It is only by climbing up a long long way
That we can see the glory.
Or by bending down
Under the yellow mountain ash
To see the smallest drop of water
Fresh from the night's dew
Resting on one tiny bit of moss.

If only we could be like
Those mountains, grand,
Or that drop of water
Resting until it disappears
Into the warming day sure
To be set down
Again in the still of the night.
Our purpose would only be
To reflect the light
And that would be enough.

Sunrise slope and fog below Mount Baker, Washington. October 2004.

Joy

Yes, I am happy now.
I find joy in talking with strangers,
Smiling at the sparkling sea,
Listening to the sound of waves
And voices near me.
I find joy in seeing old friends
Regardless of the years
Of silence.

Now, I want to talk about life,
About what it's like to
Wake in the Springtime sun
And gentle morning rain,
About the way children
Love to run and take
In unexpected gifts,
Ready to receive again and
Again and again.

Ananda Marga School. Nairobi, Kenya. March 2004.

Too fast action

When I do vision,
As quickly as I get it,
My pulse races,
I tighten my head,
Worry about how to pull it off,
And promptly overwhelm myself

Then sadden me that I have failed.

Suppose I tried another course?
In winter's hold I'd wait, wait in the growing
fullness of possibility which is so distinct from
action.

By waiting, the vision grows in potency,
strength, and wisdom
Until, like spring's demand of blossoms,
The action arises
Unstoppable.

No belt, no hat, and will I be late for breakfast?

I have achieved what people
Have sought for millennia!
I can travel time and
Still not be here, now.
In this moment, I, just plain me
Have both the past and the future
In the rear view mirror of my life!

I rushed around so fast the other day,
I forgot that which holds up my pants;
That which shields from sun and snow.
Even more astounding,
I lay here pining on the past
And in the same moment made up a story
About missing breakfast tomorrow!

What?
There is little now in me.
I fear the future as if I know what already
happened there and resent the past
Because of what did.

Oh for NOW, that moment of all possibility,
The NOW of time where we may mould
the Future in spite of yesterday
And create tomorrow.

Earth Homework. Monument Valley, Utah. August 1995.

Earth Homework, Summer 95

Look: Underneath our hurriedness.
The earth moves, time is eons.
Rock bends, folds back upon itself,
Washes clean in long flowing water.

She was made before us,
Lies deep beneath the forest floor,
Bears all of us with sweet support.

Linger here a very long time.
See?
She moves grain by grain,
Washed away, set down again—
Mountain becomes plain,
Plain is cut to gorge,
Sea floor rolls, folds, pushes,
Births mountains.

Tired of your hurriedness?
Go home. stay put.
Earth will be there, still flowing
Like solid rock.

If only we stayed still
Long enough to be so carved,
Settled down grain by unique small grain
And hardened by pressure long endured,
Yet soft enough to be formed by sacred
water and wind exposing our essence,
Then washed away in utter silence.

Sunrise at Kiluea

Pele prepared us for morning,
Her long swirling hair
Lying about in braids
Of black and silver.

She awoke in glowing red,
Moving down the mountain
At her own pace, dripping
Into the sea who
Waited patiently, vastly
For her arrival.

We were there at dawn
When glowing earth and sun
Reached out in unity
Across space and water.

Today they seemed of one element—
Fierce creation of the new day.

Slow creation

I seem to emerge haltingly
from deep within my soul
as Kiluea moves inch by inch.
Glowing hot one moment
crusted over the next
until heat rises again
and cracks open my cooled spirit.

I break apart
pieces flying off
as the molten core of my being
moves again—
a few feet.

Must my unfolding be so stubborn,
moving with red hot intensity only
from time to time?
Could I not move with steady
rhythm like the sea,
each wave arriving
in predicable succession?

And yet
for all that movement
the sea is only
shaped by land
not by herself,
and within that form
she remains unchanged,
created once at the
beginning of time
then standing witness
to earth's slow birth.

This morning
a few feet of earth emerged
in fire.

Knowing now what violence
it took for God
to make the world
in only seven days,
I resist my own creation.

Birth of Earth. Kiluea Volcano, Hawaii. February 2005.

Rebirth

Now I climb out of my own darkness.

My heart beat quickens
Like it did in my mother's womb.
Still not a complete person
But conscious and beating,
Blood flowing life.

Life as keen as the first life,
The first quickening
From that moment
Before the beat
To the first pulse
– a world, a universe apart.

Seasonal cousins

Do winter and spring know each other?
Their energies are so different
They seem to be from different parents.

The deep winter soul stands
Quietly unknowing whether to live or fly,
While spring's rising light and sap
Energy seep out filling the void,
Spilling over flooding rushing
Noisily shouting haza!

Like relatives from different coasts
They know they are part of one
Extended family and yet
Are not quite sure
How they could be related.

But from creator's view they are so close
One flows from the other, and
Should spring upstage her elder sister,
The cold one may come back with vengeance.
Jealous sibling!

They must be related.
Blossoms peek out of snow
Just before full flower.

Harvest

As we have moved farther and farther from the land, one of the greatest casualties is our understanding and appreciation of the harvest. Where I grew up, the air grew sweet with ripe fruit and hay at the end of the growing season. The biggest event of the year was the county fair where all sorts of the results of labor were shown. That old fashioned gathering became for me a kind of ritual and even now reminds me that we must pay special attention to results. But not in our "outcome oriented" ways.

There is much emphasis on results today, but I think the second aspect of harvest is sorely lacking. That part is the savoring and celebrating of the past cycle from seed planting, through careful maturation and finally to full ripeness and gathering in. We seek results so much it is as if we would will them into existence untouched by human sweat.

These poems arrived for me during one or another activity related to the cycle and call, I hope, for us to once again notice how the harvest came to be and how much sweeter the fruit is if we stop to taste it.

In the harvest, there is also recognition that our own lives will be harvested in good time. And that is bitter sweet.

The Burden of Abundance

The apples trees hang heavy with fruit this year.
And in the abundance of the harvest,
Branches groan with its weight.
Limbs uplifted in the
Spring touch the ground.

Were it not for the harvest surely the limbs
Would finally break in their abundance
and the fruit be wasted, rotting on the ground.

Are we so burdened?
Do we even notice
What is ripening with in us?
Are we attentive to
What is already sweet
In our lives,
Or do our true riches
Go unsavored, weighing
Us down at once and then rotting
In passing time.

Is not our growing hunger some how related to
Always wanting more and not digesting
What we have?

Crowds of people suffocate, buried under
Our wealth and wanting more
While children arrive at school
Without breakfast.

We are so worried about starvation
We fail to notice the manna
Lying at our feet.

The Executor

What honor this –
To gather in our father's life,
His harvest,
The nourishment he gave—
Fulfilled that we might carry on.

Now I, distributor,
Gather in his essence,
Much more than gold,
And pass it on.

It is also I who carry
The ashes of his life
Up the mountains he loved.

Such sweet burden
To nourish them on his behalf.

Tears fall now and soon from winter skies.

*Photo credit:
John P. Magill.
Bridalveil
Falls, Yosemite
National Park.*

All in good time

Now the apples are ready.
True, I pruned and watered;
I trapped bugs.
But all that was simply to allow
Space for the blossom
To become an apple.
I did not make the tree, the water
The blossom, the fruit.
I did not make the sun
Or leaves or invent
The photosynthesis.
No, I am merely
Witness to this holy
Ground, this cycle
Made by God.

I wanted to harvest two weeks ago when
It was more convenient.
That was not to be.
When fruit is ready we harvest
And not a day sooner.
Each tree in its variety, like us,
will take its own sweet time.

Harvest Timing

The apples are gathered in now
And it was a good crop.
The last of the raspberries
Mould on the canes,
A few tomatoes linger
In hopes of one more sunny day.

It's been a good garden this year.
I've spent more time than ever
Weeding beds, mowing, trimming;
I even attacked the blackberries
And morning glory vines.

Weeks ago I noticed progress in
My cleaning out, but yesterday
I saw these last ones
Have not given up.
New vines, even in September,
Creep back into the walks,
Set off new shoots into the Rhododendrons.

Now I see life in a mix of ripe fruit
And work that isn't done.
Come Spring, I'll hit the vines again
And feel I've made more progress –
Once more cutting back the over growth
Pulling up the morning glory
secretly invading the vegetables.
Every year I cut them back,
And they in turn grow more.

Life, then, is as much about
The weeds as it is about the fruit.
As ministers, stewards of the garden,
We weed and prune,
Sometimes getting what we want.
The cuttings, handled well,
Turn to compost for growing
More sweet fruit.

Dangerous Lunch

I never knew getting a sandwich
could be dangerous, but learned so
as I walked to Subway for a bit of bread,
Of cheese and of salami.

One step more and I
Would have been crushed
Like so much pepper
Or plate glass and frames
Lying in small chards and twisted steel.

The guilty truck had no reverse
But I found mine and quickly
Stepped back—
Glass at my feet—
Smoking tires—
A last clunk of broken steel
Crashing to the floor.

Odd how thin the veil
Between a sandwich and death.
No more complaining about
Lack of adventure.
Life is hot enough.
Hold the onions
And the jalapenos!

YES

This morning I am saying yes.

Perhaps success is simply embracing
This moment, these sounds, this full heart.
If this is what life most asks of us,
Then I am full.

I am saying yes to waking up today,
To seeing early morning light and quiet streets.
Yes to the men who seem
To have slept on the beach,
Now joining in the café,
Sharing coffee and the local paper,
Greeting one another in familiar tones.

Yes to the people sitting alone
With coffee and a morning muffin
Starting their days,
And to the bright eyed woman
Making coffee with friendly greetings.

Yes to the little girl sitting on mom's lap,
Hands mingled, smiling.
Yes to the look of concerned,
Furrowed brows over mom's eyes
Hidden by dark glasses.
Her day also is starting just as it is.

Anada Marga School. Nairobi, Kenya. March 2004.

And yes to the old songs on the radio
Played in this beach side place for decades.

Yes to my day already in motion
And to each person I meet.
Yes to life, to our common goal of living.

You, dear friend,
Where is your YES today?

Index of first lines